CW00341271

1,000,000 Books

are available to read at

www.ForgottenBooks.com

Read online
Download PDF
Purchase in print

ISBN 978-0-259-50641-6
PIBN 10820641

This book is a reproduction of an important historical work. Forgotten Books uses
state-of-the-art technology to digitally reconstruct the work, preserving the original format
whilst repairing imperfections present in the aged copy. In rare cases, an imperfection in
the original, such as a blemish or missing page, may be replicated in our edition. We do,
however, repair the vast majority of imperfections successfully; any imperfections that
remain are intentionally left to preserve the state of such historical works.

Forgotten Books is a registered trademark of FB &c Ltd.
Copyright © 2018 FB &c Ltd.
FB &c Ltd, Dalton House, 60 Windsor Avenue, London, SW19 2RR.
Company number 08720141. Registered in England and Wales.

For support please visit www.forgottenbooks.com

1 MONTH OF
FREE
READING

at
www.ForgottenBooks.com

By purchasing this book you are eligible for one month membership to ForgottenBooks.com, giving you unlimited access to our entire collection of over 1,000,000 titles via our web site and mobile apps.

To claim your free month visit:
www.forgottenbooks.com/free820641

* Offer is valid for 45 days from date of purchase. Terms and conditions apply.

English
Français
Deutsche
Italiano
Español
Português

www.forgottenbooks.com

Mythology Photography **Fiction**
Fishing Christianity **Art** Cooking
Essays Buddhism Freemasonry
Medicine **Biology** Music **Ancient
Egypt** Evolution Carpentry Physics
Dance Geology **Mathematics** Fitness
Shakespeare **Folklore** Yoga Marketing
Confidence Immortality Biographies
Poetry **Psychology** Witchcraft
Electronics Chemistry History **Law**
Accounting **Philosophy** Anthropology
Alchemy Drama Quantum Mechanics
Atheism Sexual Health **Ancient History**
Entrepreneurship Languages Sport
Paleontology Needlework Islam
Metaphysics Investment Archaeology
Parenting Statistics Criminology
Motivational

"O winds that blow across sea, what is the story that bring . . ."

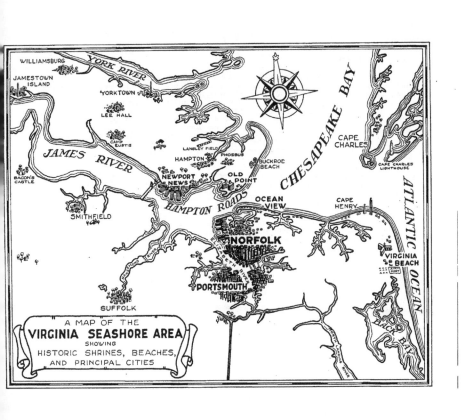

A MAP OF THE
VIRGINIA SEASHORE AREA
SHOWING
HISTORIC SHRINES, BEACHES,
AND PRINCIPAL CITIES

THE foreshore of Virginia, the Dune Country as John Richard Moreland, its poet, has so well named it, along with the connecting coast of North Carolina, is one of the wildest, most naturally beautiful, most unchanged regions of our Atlantic seaboard. Although it was the first to bear the footprints of English settlers; although railroads, boulevards, steamship and aeroplane lines bring its magic of sea and wind-tossed dunes to the doorsteps of half the nation; although in the heart of it, amid the whisper of pines and ceaseless roar of surf, there has grown up a great resort at Virginia Beach, the primitive freedom of this Dune Country is still untouched, aye, almost unchanged. For what are a host of people, what, even, many miles of hotels and cottages, of civilization, to the unmeasured emptiness of horizons marked here by unresting waves, there by league on league of drifted sand? Tracks do not live long in the ocean. Wind and tide silently sweep them away on shore. Footprints of yesterday become one with those of 300 years; and wave and dune of tomorrow will not be different from those that lifted here when America was young.

Even if you are living in this pleasant resort, relaxing in its comforts, tasting its delicious foods, finding renewed vigor in its broad variety of entertainment, all of these things are swept clear of your mind, like marks in sand by a rising tide. when you turn your eyes to the sea . . . to the long breakers rolling out of its unknown depths . . . to the wild, wild bursts of spray curving, leaping, swirling, until the world is flecked with them. It becomes apparent then that this resort is only a veneer, though withal a charming one, on the majesty of this endless struggle of sea and land for mastery.

Away from Virginia Beach there is not even this veneer. The sandy battlefield is stripped of everything, as it has been from the beginning, except the elemental forces of wind and sea and earth . . . and unconquerable life. Back of the fresh, untracked shore, washed by each tide as clean as eternity of any print of Time, the dunes rear high and lonely under a tangle of sassafras, wild plum, sword grass and jasmine. In places, as at Cape Henry, they wrench free of their matted covering and join the forces of death in an irresistible, amazing march inland over forest and swamp and field.

A wind's in the heart of me, a fire's in my heels,
I am tired of brick and stone and rumbling wagon-wheels;
I hunger for the sea's edge, the limits of the land,
Where the wild old Atlantic is shouting on the sand.
                    —A Wanderer's Song, Masefield.

HOWEVER, as the resort of Virginia Beach is only a veneer on the dunes, so are the dunes themselves, with all their majesty, only the fringe of a mightier presence. Beyond the Sand is the Sea. All that lives or is bears its impress. Out of it life was born . . . Into it life returns. . . .

In resort or dune you can find whatever your heart may desire or get away from what you will. But ever in your ears will beat the roar of the sea, ever will the wind fling its spray into your face, never will you be able for a moment to forget that over this Dune Country, as over all it touches, there rules a force as elemental, as powerful, as life itself.

It colors the wind and sky and days. During the long happy sunlight hours and first rich ones of the moon, it tugs at your being until there is naught to do but come watch the dreams and mysteries it rolls up from beyond the horizon. To watch . . . and to learn, perhaps, as Elbert Hubbard learned before going down to its depths on his last long journey:

"The sea knows all things, for at night when the winds are asleep the stars confide to him their secrets. In his breast are stored away all the elements that go to make up the round world. Beneath . . . lie buried the sunken kingdoms of fable and legend. . . .

"It is not to be wondered that men have worshipped the ocean, for in its depths they have seen mirrored the image of Eternity—of Infinity. . . .

"Men have fallen on their faces to worship the sea. Women have thrown him their children to appease his wrath. . . .

"And what does the sea do with all these secrets, mysteries and treasures? Go shrive thyself, and with soul all in tune to the harmonies of the Universe, listen to the waves and they shall tell thee the secrets of life."

But all watches must have an end; all secrets are not learned in a day. Sometime far in the late hours, when the moon is high and small above a sea of glittering white, you will return to the four walls of your room to drift into dreamless sleep, of which the last memory, through the rhythmic minor notes of night animals, will be the throb and dying hush of breaking waves rolling up over consciousness like the foam of a rising tide.

THE CALL

Some like the noise of the city,
With its rattle and clatter and clang;
They like trolley cars with their jolts and their jars
Or they favor the city-bred gang.

They like to nose-dive in the subway,
Or to shuffle along with the crowd;
But, Man! It's the sea that's a-calling to me—
And the call never sounded so loud..

VIRGINIA BEACH is perhaps the most fortunately placed ocean resort in the country. Half our Atlantic coast extends to the north, half to the south, so that visitors from Atlanta or Jacksonville or New Orleans can reach it as easily as their brethren from New York or Boston or Chicago—and none be ever far removed from home. Half the country can thus conveniently and logically look to it as its focus of recreation—re-creation, let us say, as the word was originally—of health and vigor and mental freshness.

It is as if the Dune Country had been formed with such a purpose in mind. From Willoughby Spit and Ocean View on the Chesapeake, around Cape Henry in one great sweep far beyond the Carolina line there is nothing but sand and sea and sky. There is no such thing as "a white curve of beach in a rocky bay" or "a low, sandy spit running out from the rough foreland." The scale is too vast for that. All the long coast is a song of the loneliness and beauty of tide-swept sand. It is as if the whole ocean had rolled up here an offering to fill the need of millions. And in the center of this great stretch of low shoreline, touched with the dun, and grey, and white, of sand, and mist, and wind-whipped spray, is Virginia Beach.

In the early warm days of May bathers begin to congregate on its ever clean and beautiful sands. By mid-summer it is a surge of color not only along the two miles of modern cement and steel "boardwalk" but as well in front of cottages spreading as far again up the beach. Thousands laze in the sand; thousands more linger in the water or ride the manes of white sea horses, the magnificent surf, galloping in from the open Atlantic.

Autumn, spring, or winter, any is a season that seen by itself might cause you to believe that its days here are the best of all. But of all the year the days of happiness and peace are the summer days. As you lie on the white, sun-bathed beach with the sapphire of sparkling waves curling up to break into a million fragments of crystal at your feet, it is not difficult to forget that time exists, nor to drowse and dream and hope that such days will never end.

During the three summer months, whatever can bloom,
  blooms.
Besides the three summer months, oh, there are no flowers.
   . . . .
In this one life-time, whatever can be happy, is happy.
Enjoy this one life-time as ever you can enjoy it.
                      —Tibetan Song.

I
T is enough on such a beach to have the sand and sea and sun. With them, and the dreaming blue sky, any bit of it becomes a pleasant one. But here and there man has even improved it, as at the Cavalier Beach Club. Here, in summer, a fairy wand touches the sand and out of the dunes there arises, not a stone's throw from the sea, a magic little city.

When the afternoon sun dips low, sending long shadows down from the dunes, this becomes like some fabled shore of the Argonauts, as, above the murmur of voices, soft music weaves an undertone through the ripple and crash and dying swish of each wave that comes and goes. Many dance. But many more cannot leave off looking at the sea, where each wave is a new picture.

Beyond the line of surf there rises now and then a school of dolphins. Rhythmically, gracefully, they arch in and out of the water as they pass, the Gentlemen Adventurers of the sea, following a wanderlust that will not be stilled.

Farther offshore are man-made sea-wanderers: Perhaps a coasting schooner, its white sails silhouetted like clouds against the sky, a phantom from a past that was billowy with these creatures of wind and water . . . perhaps a trim, knife-like liner slipping along . . . perhaps an ancient tramp battered by the winds and storms of all the seven seas, patched and ragged, dark with red lead and rust, but still plodding as it will ever plod even when it sinks on some roaring moonless night by slow, tenacious inches into a maddened sea.

Or above the horizon perhaps there hangs a smudge to tell of a ship that passes beyond the edge of the world. Long and low and filled with the wistfulness of a hand lifted in farewell it lingers, slowly drifts away, becomes a wisp . . . is gone.

And there comes over him who watches the feeling that he has seen a shadow of these happy days by the sea. Too soon they will be gone . . . too soon be only memories of which he may feel as do the northern Chinese of the blue warmth of their summer that leads so swiftly into the hopeless desolation of winter: "When these days are gone, there will be no others left in the world."

*"It takes women longer to learn to swim than men be-
cause men have to teach themselves."*

I

F you are not content with the shoreline and shifting picture of the sea; if the ways of the sand-crab or curious sand-flea, or gull, sometime fail to absorb, turn any way you wish and there will be something to do. It may be salt water fishing off Virginia Beach, in Lynnhaven and Chesapeake Bays, or in quiet, beautiful landlocked stretches of tide water. Again, if you prefer, your hook may be dropped in fresh-water lakes between the beach and Norfolk. Close at hand are boardwalk attractions and the salt water pools which, curiously, are always filled whether the sea is stormy or smooth. Canoes and sailboats wind between pine-fringed shores. Dunes and beach and Cape Henry Desert invite hiker and horseback rider. An open air arena brings nights of rare boxing and wrestling. Golfing, tennis, archery, trap-shooting, hunting—each is delightful enough to want to crowd the days with itself alone. Magic Dismal Swamp hovers only a few miles in the background. A few more to the south, by beach or road, are Roanoke Island and Kitty Hawk, each a chapter in the saga of man's eternal quest for the unknown: the one of Raleigh's immortal Lost Colony and the mysterious word it left the world—"Croatan;" the other of the Wrights and the ceaseless wind at Kitty Hawk.

At Cape Henry and Jamestown are memories of the first permanent English colony. At Norfolk, Yorktown, Richmond, Lynnhaven, Williamsburg—almost wherever you step in this history filled birthplace of America other tremendous and vital events have taken place. Even Virginia Beach has a fragment of the past in the place-name "Sea Tack," which is derived from the "Sea Attack," or bombardment suffered by this section in the War of 1812.

Fort Story, Fortress Monroe, the Navy Yard, the Naval Base, busy Hampton Roads—a summer might be filled with looking, if you could drag yourself away from Virginia Beach.

If you do leave at times for a day, you always return for the nights. They are filled with music—for those who wish it that of the dance; for others, the whispering song of the stars and the sea shining like grey satin under the moon and far away, out of the darkness, golden blurs of ship lights with Cape Henry's guiding beacon unceasingly, rhythmically, kindly, flashing its friendly hail.

"So he crossed himself and ejaculated honestly enough,
'Lord, turn away mine eyes lest they behold vanity!' · · ·
and looked nevertheless."—Hypatia, Charles Kingsley.

BLOW THE MAN DOWN

As I was a-cruising down a Norfolk street,
To my, yeo-ho! blow the man down!
A pretty young damsel I chanced for to meet,
O, give us some time to blow the man down!

She was round in the counter and bluff in the bow,
To my, yeo-ho! blow the man down!
So I took in all sail and cried "Way enough now!"
O, give us some time to blow the man down!

I dipped her my topsail and took her in tow,
To my, yeo-ho! blow the man down!
And yardarm to yardarm away we did go,
O, give us some time to blow the man down!

But as we departed she said unto me,
To my, yeo-ho! blow the man down!
"There's a spanking full-rigger just ready for sea.
O, give us some time to blow the man down!

That spanking full-rigger for Rio was bound,
To my, yeo-ho! blow the man down!
She was very-well manned and very well found,
O, give us some time to blow the man down!

But as soon as that packet was clear of the bar,
To my, yeo-ho! blow the man down!
The mate knocked me down with the end of a spar,
O, give us some time to blow the man down!

As soon as that packet was out on the sea.
To my, yeo-ho! blow the man down!
'Twas devilish hard treatment of every degree,
O, give us some time to blow the man down!

So I give you fair warning before we belay,
To my, yeo-ho! blow the man down!
Don't never take no heed of what pretty girls say,
O, give us some time to blow the man down!

—Old Halliard Chanty.

Time, it is well known, sometimes flies like a bird, some-
times crawls like a worm, but man is wont to be particularly
happy when he does not even notice whether it passes quickly
or slowly.—Turgenev.

NOWHERE in the country will a golfer's heart throb more rapidly than just back of the dunes and beating surf of Virginia's seashore. Out of the forest his paradise has been carved. Like great avenues, traced with the slender shadows of trees, fairways wind in and away from vistas of blue, sparkling bays. On knolls and in pleasant nooks greens await—at times for long, when even the most enthusiastic player forgets his game in the wonder of a cardinal streaking in crimson glory across the sky; or lingers to listen again and again to a mournful, thrilling "whip-poor-will" echoing from the dark pines.

The sun is hot, brilliantly hot, as Dixie suns are ever, but it does not depress or enervate like city heat. The heady tang of pine, the rich odor of forest mould, the freshness of air swept clean over blue waves and through green leaves, set the heart atingle. Energy wells up without end. Muscles become eager for action. Nerves are relaxed. After hours of playing, whatever the physical weariness, vitality is undiminished, spirits are buoyant, and you are ready, with just a step through forest and dune, to plunge into the cool, foaming crest of a breaking wave.

There are two such courses at Virginia Beach, famous throughout golfdom—the Princess Anne and the Cavalier.

Of the former, whose picturesque first tee is shown, Walter Hagen has been quoted as saying: "The Princess Anne course is of real championship caliber . . . " It "presents a wonderful variety of holes calling for all kinds of shots, bringing into play every club in one's bag. The rolling fairways, flanked by tall, stately pines, present a beautiful picture."

He might have added that the roar of breaking waves sounds a majestic, soothing undertone throughout a match, now dying away when the sea calms or the wind shifts offshore or the course winds into the pines toward Little Neck Creek . . . now booming out its insistent, vibrant melody as the last five holes are followed little more than a quarter of a mile from the shore.

This beautiful and enticingly difficult course has each year grown in favor as increasing numbers of golfers, professional and amateur, have tasted its charm and gone away to vouch for it to every audience they could find.

Nor is its fame based merely on the tales of summer visitors. Autumn and spring have beauty not to be found even in glorious summer days. And in the winter months, tempered as they are by winds off the Gulf Stream, golf may be played here when more northern courses, and even those of the same latitude, are shivering under snow and ice.

A rule of three I give to thee,
If thou wouldst good golfer be:
Cultivate a memory poor, or lie the more,
Or ever divide with goodly denominator!

                               —Tee Wiles.

THE "Lake" or Eleventh Hole of the Cavalier Golf Club is a jewel set among the trees. In its lake is miniatured the procession of delight awaiting the voyager around this course where every hole is different, every fairway opens up unexpected beauties of landscape and bold, challenging hazards. From the Country Club on Linkhorn Bay, the course weaves around the many estuaries of Little Neck Creek, crosses at the Twelfth Hole to Great Neck Creek and continues its route near the water until, at the Eighteenth, Linkhorn Bay is again reached, and the whole of lovely Bird Neck Point has been covered.

In such a superb setting it was not difficult to eliminate any sign of monotony or sameness. Each hole has its own personality, and many of them are made similar, in their own unique way, to famous holes of other courses. The Lake Hole is a replica of the Eleventh "at Saint Andrews, the 13th at the National and the original at the Lido." Number Two is the twin of number One at the National. Number Five does not differ greatly from the well known Biarritz one-shot hole, nor number Seven from a like hole at Garden City; while lying between is the huge punch-bowl of number Six, whose likeness is Fox Chapel of the Chicago Golf Club.

The Tenth can be matched at Lido and the Fourteenth at the roadside hole of Saint Andrews. The Eighteenth, nestling on a tiny cape near the clubhouse, has its counterpart in the famous Redin hole at North Berwick, Scotland, but has a superior nowhere—which, for that matter, may be said of the course as well.

Someone has written, 'Few good intentions come to so bad an end as those of a golfer.' But the one that leads you here for golf happiness on a golden afternoon is certainly not one of these.

You have heard the beat of the offshore wind
And the thresh of the deep-sea rain;
You have heard the song—how long! how long!
Pull out on the trail again!

—L'Envoi, Kipling.

T HERE are some who never tire of the edge of the sea. Each wave to them is a new poem, a troubador come from afar with strange and thrilling tales of mysteries beyond the horizon. In learning the ways of gull or sandpiper or sand-fiddler, they find a knowledge, wisdom perhaps, that books cannot tell. For them life on the beach has endless variety and a summer at the seashore is truly that and nothing else.

Yet it may be you are one of the many who want only a few hours in the white sands. You hunger for other adventure . . . And where better can you find it than on a spirited horse roving gypsy-free with the wind!

Like the wind you wander where you will—perhaps inland by quiet waters; perhaps to the great stretch of empty, wind-carved dunes, the ancient *moving dunes* back of Cape Henry; perhaps behind them in turn to "The Desert" of forest and sand and swamp in which, except for the many miles of trails, there is little sign of change since the days of John Smith.

Whatever the month, "The Desert" is a song of color. Dogwood and wild plum, jasmine and bayberry, poplar and field maple, oak and pine, each has its tint and its season. Even in winter there lifts out of the swamp and white, rolling sand a certain stark beauty of bare hardwoods and dark green pines silhouetted against the steely sky.

To these the trails will lead, and then, as the setting sun flames crimson through the pine tops, there may be a wild, thundering ride down the packed sands of the tide line. For mile on mile the glistening beach unrolls, the churned white edge of each advancing wave is spattered aside by flying hoofs, the surf breaks tumultously almost on top you, and in the wet sands where waves recede with soft whispers of dying foam, like wind through dry leaves, there is mirrored you and fleeing horse and golden clouds in the west.

The return, with purple shadows and the first pin-pricks of stars moving in changing procession up the wet sands, now mistily clear, now swallowed in a rushing wave, is like a journey along the edge of some old, old mythical sea . . . is. if ever was, the perfect ending of a perfect day.

We are told that "the Reverend Anthony Walke ministered the Word of Life in this venerable sanctuary (Old Donation Church) according to the forms of the Episcopal Church . . ." But an old story comes back to us which is not a matter of court record . . . . Should the sound of the horns and cry of the hounds be heard during any part of the service, down got Parson Walke out of the Chancel, mounted his horse tied in the churchyard, and was off after the fox with the best of them, leaving the Clerk, Mr. Dick Edwards, to finish the service.—Down on Old Lynnhaven, Mrs. Philip Alexander Bruce.

F OR more than 300 years white men have hunted game in Tidewater Virginia; and for centuries before them the Indian found here such a wealth of wild life that his dreams of a Happy Hunting Ground must have ever seemed close to fulfillment.

The section is still for sportsmen one of the Happy-Hunting Grounds of America. On Back Bay, south of Virginia Beach, and beyond into Currituck Sound, great flights of duck and geese wing down from grey northern skies in autumn. Each season they gather in such numbers, despite the depletion of recent years, that there is hardly a hunter who has not as his major itch the desire to come once to these waters in search of "canvas back," and, if he has been, to come back again.

The art of "turkey calling" has not passed. Natives can still, as in the old days, lead you to a bag of wild turkey, or at least to a shot at these magnificent bronzed birds, by imitating their cry. And all the lesser feather tribe, including pheasant and fat, unexcelled quail, roam in great numbers through the marshes, dunes and low, rich farmlands.

Deer are abundant in the Great Dismal Swamp, as are black bear, whether or not one is on the hunt for them. Many a skin of bruin is carried away each fall as proof of the prowess, if not *all* the tales, of mighty huntsmen.

But the sport of sports to Virginians, and to some preachers, is the hue and cry after Master Reynard. Some of the earliest records are tales of hunting him. And today the winding of horns, the deep, musical baying of hounds, the thunder of hoofs, still sound across the rolling lowlands like the echoing memory of old Lynnhaven days . . . still tugs sinfully, no doubt, at the hearts of godly ministers who would teach The Word and yet would fain follow the example of Parson Walke and joyously chase the devil incarnate in foxy Reynard.

THE SEA-ROADS

The Seven Seas lie wide and deep
    And far their pathways lead, and wide;
We shall not know what dead things sleep
    Beneath their waves nor what they hide;

We shall not know the ships that lie
    Deep sunk upon their shifting floors
Nor whose the ghosts that flit and fly
    Upon their thousand-sided shores.

Nay, these things shall we never know
    'Nor where the trackless pathways lead,
But ever when the sea-winds blow
    We shall obey, our hearts shall heed;

And out into the roaring seas,
    Past all traditions' graves and fears,
Our ships shall answer their decrees
    And follow them across the years.
              —*J. F. Dahlgren.*

To many Americans their navy is a mere word of politicians or an expensive toy that should be discarded. But it will never again be such a little thing to any one of them once he has seen from a lonely dune a squadron of lean, grey destroyers sweep above the horizon, swing neatly into line despite waves heeling them to their beam-ends, and round Cape Henry for home after months of wandering in distant seas. As he looks, something within him is stirred. He remembers John Paul Jones bearding England on her home shores with a single ship. He sees again the French fleet that off this very cape made possible our victory at Yorktown. Before him float *Old Ironsides* and her famous breed, the clumsy Monitor, the Flying Squadron of 1898, the host of ships that by unswerving faithfulness in convoy and patrol brought about victory in our last war. And slowly there comes the realization that we, the only great country with unrestricted coast-lines on the world's two greatest oceans, are a nation of the sea, that out of the sea we were born at spray-wet Cape Henry itself, that on it—for history does repeat itself—our very life may sometime again be at stake.

When the fleet is here in January, spring or autumn, Hampton Roads is dotted with grey ships. But at even other times there is not a week, hardly a day, that a restless grey wanderer does not pass the Chesapeake Capes; for back of them, in Hampton Roads and adjacent waters, is the most strategically important part of the coast and therefore the center of naval activities. These are largely concentrated at the Norfolk Naval Base on Hampton Roads and the Navy Yard on Elizabeth River. Both are the busiest in the East. At the Base are headquarters for the Fifth Naval District, a large training station for recruits, the distribution point for fleet supplies, the maintenance center for Atlantic Fleet aircraft, a school for aviation training, a large submarine base, and other activities.

The Navy Yard, with one of the world's largest dry-docks and a fourth of the country's total, with shipbuilding equipment and unexcelled repair facilities, never fails to have several ships in its docks. He who has not visited a naval vessel should go aboard one of these not merely to see their uniqueness and cleanliness and efficiency, but to be amazed as well by the utilization of space from topmast to keel that in a battleship 500 to 600 feet long and only 100 feet wide provides 1000 to 1500 men with living quarters, postoffice, tailor, laundry, stores of several kinds, barbers, soda fountain, cobbler, hospital, movies, carpenters, repair shops, blacksmith, offices of every sort, most of the other necessities of a modern city . . . and yet has enough space left over for the armor, the power and grim fighting equipment, the preparation and training, to steam out in battle line on green, wind-lashed seas to save our nation—if we as a nation have not neglected its needs—as its forebears have done so gloriously and so often in the past.

Catfish swimmin' in de water,
Nigger wid a hook an' line,
Says de catfish, "Look here, nigger man,
You ain' got me dis time!"

I'll eat when I'm hungry, I'll drink when I'm dry,
And if the Yankees don't ketch me, I'll live till I die.
—Old Rebel Song.

I F *Resurrection the Lord be Praised George Washington Abraham Brown*, "Riz" for short, can catch them, so can you. They are there, millions of them in bay and sea and inland waters waiting for your hook. You can haul them in from the pier at Virginia Beach or offshore from boats. On Linkhorn Bay, at Lynnhaven Inlet, and at Ocean View on Chesapeake Bay there are hundreds of other boats ready with bait, tackle and lines to take you out for an hour's or a day's sport. Spot and croaker, bass and bluefish, weakfish or sea trout and porgy, drum and many others are ready not only to give you a sporty battle but to fill your plate as well, when you have returned to your home kitchen, with as delicious a food as you have ever eaten. There is hardly a day in which you will not have fair luck; and to make up for the few times the fish are off on a vacation there are some days when you can't haul them in fast enough, when you might look very much like "Riz," even to the sunburn, walking home with your catch.

If you prefer fresh water angling, there are lakes only a few miles away on the Norfolk road. License, bait, tackle, boatsman and boat are on hand; pike, pickerel and perch are waiting for you; and lurking in deep water is that delight of all fishermen who love a gamey opponent, the large mouthed bass.

Once you have tasted the joys of this sport, if for no other reason, there will not a summer pass without your boarding a train for Virginia Beach, on which down the speeding miles this chorus will run again and again through your mind to the beat of the wheels on the rails—

Come all ye bold fishermen, listen to me
While I sing to you a song of the sea . . .
Then blow ye winds westerly, westerly blow,
We're bound to the south'ard, so steady we go.

—The Song of the Fishes.

The site of Norfolk, with its wonderful
and its nearness to the ocean, from the earl
American Colonies, has been marked by stude
geography as a spot designed by nature to
world's greatest ports.—Norfolk Ledger-Dis[
of Tidewater Virginia.

Hampton Roads with its adjacent waterways forms America's finest natural harbor. Each year, especially since the World War when its boundless facilities were so urgently needed, it has grown in use and importance until now nearly every hour of the day is marked by one or many ships slipping down the channel through the outermost capes. To the west, the Roads run naturally into the broad mouth of James River, and it in turn, to the south, into that of the Elizabeth River. It is on this semi-peninsula, on the Roads, two rivers and many inlets, invitingly open by land to the south and west, that the city and great port of Norfolk has grown up not twenty miles from the place of the first landing at Cape Henry.

Across the Elizabeth River, and practically a continuation of Norfolk, is Portsmouth. Although the two cities, with a combined population of close on to 200,000, form a thriving commercial and industrial center, there is much else in them of interest and much inconspicuous beauty. In Portsmouth are early homes and churches, the restful, lovely grounds of the Naval Hospital set on a low point of land jutting out into the harbor, the Navy Yard with its relic-filled park in the old section and always alongside its piers a number of trim grey fighting vessels. In Norfolk are City Hall Avenue, illustrated on the opposite page, and other streets where still lingers something of the charm of ante-bellum days. At Fort Norfolk; in the cloistered churchyard of old Saint Paul's, the only building left standing when Norfolk was bombarded and burned early in the Revolutionary War; among the old homes and beautiful gardens on Botetourt and Freemason and other streets; in outlying parts of the city where, on inlet and stream, uncrowded, flower-sheltered residential districts have developed — in every elm-shaded street and myrtle-hidden corner there is much of beauty both old and new that most visitors passing through the busy downtown section never see and never imagine to be present.

Norfolk also has the distinction of having within its city limits, and only eight miles from its center, Ocean View on Chesapeake Bay, one of the largest and most popular resorts in the country. With its fine bay swimming, its fishing, the beautiful new Nansemond Hotel, its amusement parks, golfing, and many other attractions, it helps to make life happier for many thousands every hot summer's day.

But to him who loves the tides and sea and the ships that ply upon it, Norfolk's harbor is the most absorbing attraction. Whether crossing it by bridge, or by ferry to Portsmouth or Newport News or Old Point Comfort or Cape Charles, the long piers for ocean steamers, the churned waters, the never-ending stream of craft large and small, harbor and coastal and seagoing, fill his heart with the song of far sea-roads and bear evidence that this great harbor may some day as it does already in certain commodities, rank foremost among all the ports of the country.

First came the bluefish, awagging his tail,
   He came up on deck and yells, "All hands make sail!"

Next came the porpoise, with his short snout,
   He jumped on the bridge and yells, "Ready about!"

Now came the swordfish, the scourge of the sea,
   The order that he gave is "Hellums a-lee!"

       * * *

Up jumped the fisherman, his face all a-grin,
   And with his big net he scooped them all in!
              —The Song of the Fishes.

I
F you arise early any week-day morning and walk south beyond the end of the boardwalk at Virginia Beach, you may arrive in time to see the Stormont fishing boats setting out for the pounds or returning with their silvery catch. Perhaps, even, you can arrange to go with them to watch the hauling in of the nets. If so, it will be a trip not soon to be forgotten, for the food fish they bring ashore are not by any means all the strange creatures of the depths that they lift above the waves. Ugly thorny toadfish, skates, huge sting rays, sea turtles, swordfish, sea robins, filefish, dogfish, bigeyes, crabeaters, moonfish, cowfish—the list is long and well-nigh unbelievable. Until you see for yourself the curious burden of the nets, you cannot realize the astounding forms of life existing in the sea beyond the narrow limits you reach when bathing in it.

The stakes of pounds show all along the coast past Ocean View to Willoughby Spit. But they are only one phase of the tremendous fishing industry that operates in the vicinity of the Chesapeake Capes. Trawlers ply to and from their fishing grounds 40 or 50 miles offshore. Along the beach above Ocean View, almost any summer's evening is filled with the splashing and flapping of silvery bodies as the fishermen wind in their huge nets with great, creaking windlasses. Just a step from Fortress Monroe at Phoebus and Hampton—the oldest incorporated English settlement still in existence, having been established in 1610 by colonists from Jamestown—is the outstanding hard crab and crab meat center of the country.

And who in this world has not heard of Lynnhaven and Mobjack and the other varieties of oysters that have carried the fame of this section wherever men have hungry stomachs! In fact, one of the first records of the First Colonists, set down by Captain George Percy of an incident that happened to his party probably in the vicinity of the "mountains" or sand-dunes of Lynnhaven Inlet a short while after the landing at Cape Henry, is of that still most delightful delicacy of the Virginia Coast—roasted oysters, fresh from the sea. It is while speaking of the Indian tribes encountered on an exploring trip that the Captain writes:

"We came to a place where they had made a great fire and had been newly roasting oysters. When they perceived our coming, they fled away to the mountains, and left many of the oysters in the fire. We ate some of the oysters, which were very large and delicate in taste."

SONG AGAINST GOODBY

Don't say goodby! We'll meet again somewhere,
Because good comrades always meet again . . .
Adventure always has a need for men:

*   *   *   *   *   *

We'll meet again while there's more work to do,
Ships still to sail, and other wars to fight
Where dreadful dawns assail the deafened night . . .
Go home, and rest a little, if you will;
The world's around the corner, waiting still.
Upon the sea, on land, or in the air,
As we are men, we'll meet again somewhere!

—Harry Kemp.

SOME DAY when you are returning from the lofty sandy wastes of the Moving Dunes you may be tripped by a telephone wire running along the ground and your detective sense be aroused. The line will then, no doubt, lead you a merry chase up and down hill, through sandbreaks of dead pine, across rusty railroad tracks and little used roads. But of a sudden you will look up and be repaid for your trouble by the sight of a massive powder magazine or the muzzle of a 16" gun looming so large that it is almost frightening. You could have found these more easily, of course, by going to Fort Story headquarters near Cape Henry Light but it would have been a lesser pleasure than coming upon them without warning in the desert of dunes.

During target practice, the roar of these great guns—among the most powerful we have—echoes like thunder for miles down the beach. When mimic war is on, there is a bustle near them on Cape Henry road. Tan cars and trucks rush on urgent errands. Clumsy looking caterpillars bring field pieces into action. Lean and brown and toughened by drill, the world's finest soldiers hasten to carry out the details of the plan of war being calmly worked out on a map in a quiet room by the higher command.

Only a short distance south of Virginia Beach, balancing Fort Story to the north, is the State Military Reservation and rifle range where national guard units are trained and reviewed each summer by the governor.

At Fortress Monroe on Hampton Roads are interesting and historic century old fortifications that have been modernized into one of our strongest and most vital coast defenses. Nevertheless, the old fort has managed, with its moat, broad wall, and green, well-kept grounds, to retain something of the glamour of the days when war was chivalry and romance. Whether by its guns or in its museum or beneath its walls, touched on three of the six sides by rippling waves, you feel hovering about you shadows of the past, the unhurried happy laughter of the Old South, the stirring call to battle of drums long quiet.

There or at Fort Story or at the Military Reservation you may thrill to the rhythmic swing of marching troops. But nothing will linger longer with you than the memory of some starlit night when you wandered farther than you thought up the dune-shadowed beach and far away and faint above the hushed whisper of little waves there drifted softly southward to you from Fort Story the sad, lonely, poignantly beautiful notes of taps . . .

"Out of the night a bugle blows;
Soft and clear the cadence flows;
Sweeter, stronger still it grows—
Taps is sounding.

"Sobbing low the last note goes;
No, no more the tent-light glows;
Soldier's day is at its close—
Taps has sounded."

Landed April 26, 1607
Captain Gabriel Archer   Christopher
Hon. George S. Percy   Bartholomew
Edward Maria Wingfield
With twenty-five others
Who
Calling the place
"Cape Henry"
Planted a cross
April 29, 1607

—Inscription placed u
Old Lighthouse 29
Association for Prese
ginia Antiquities.

H ERE the years have not passed. Old Cape Henry Light, the oldest national lighthouse in the country, looks down over a region not greatly changed since the century of its youth. It is one of the most unique, historic and fascinating corners of America. The wild, primitive beauty of seashore and matted dune is only a beginning. Just a step inland, rising more than 100 feet above the sea, is a great rolling, *moving* expanse of sand, the *Moving Dunes* of Cape Henry. Beneath them is a forest. At their edge, slowly being covered, and beyond, is "The Desert" of swamp and virgin forest growing out of other sand that miles farther from the shore suddenly drops in tall white hills to landlocked tide waters whose like in loveliness has not often been matched.

But there is more here, much more than even the infinite variety of nature. For three centuries these sands have watched the life blood of a nation flow by. Here beacons were burned to guide its first infant commerce. Here pirates lighted misleading ones to lure honest ships aground. Near here, in both Revolutionary and Civil Wars were fought the sea battles that saved our nation. History has left its impress in every rune of sand, but its most vibrant story, echoing down through the years, is that of the first landing . . .

❧

On 20 December, 1606, great doings were stirring on the Thames, and all the city of London from the dandies and ladies of the court to the urchins around the Tower had a magic word in their mouths. "Virginia" was being colonized again. The Great Armada was a wraith of tattered glory and wrecked ships. Raleigh's Lost Colony, too, was a phantom that echoed in weird, wild tales about tavern fires. But the ships that had returned from planting it had filled men's minds with the wonder of the New World. until now a squadron was setting out again. The city was afire with their going. Michael Drayton's new poem was being widely quoted, especially these stanzas:

> And the ambitious vine,
> Crowns with his purple mass
>   The cedars reaching high
>   To kiss the sky,
> The cypress, pine,
> And useful sassafras.
>
> And cheerfully at sea,
> Success you still entice,
>   To get the pearl and gold,
>   And ours to hold
> Virginia
> Earth's only paradise.

The grey, cold sky was filled with color, with fluttering banners, with cheers of farewell, as the 3 tiny ships carrying perhaps 160 men slipped their moorings and headed downstream with the tide. . . .

The show of land there is a white, hilly sand, like unto the Downs, and along the shores great plenty of pines and firs.—Captain John Smith.

FOUR months of wandering were to pass. Just before the end the ships almost turned back. Having left the verdant, delightful West Indies, they had headed north by west hoping to reach the Chesapeake but with *"the Mariners steering more by faith than knowledge."* Indeed, three days had gone since they had reckoned to reach land and none was yet in sight. There was much discontent; even one captain *"rather desired to bear up the helm to return to England than make further search. But God, the guider of all good actions, forcing them by extreme storm to hull all night, did drive by His Providence to their desired port. . . . "*

The day after the tempest they took soundings and on the 2nd, 3rd, and 4th days *"but we could find no ground. The five and twentieth day we sounded, and had no ground at a hundred fathom. The six and twentieth day of April, about four o'clock in the morning, we descried the land of Virginia."*

"The same day we entered into the Bay of Ches-u-pi-oc directly, without any let or hindrance. There we landed and discovered a little way. . . .

"At night, when we were going aboard, there came the savages creeping upon all fours, from the hills, like bears, with their bows in their mouths, charged us very desperately in the faces, hurt Captain Gabriel Archer in both his hands, and a sailor in two places of his body very dangerous. After they had spent their arrows and felt the sharpness of our shot, they retired into the woods with a great noise, and so left us."

For several days they lingered exploring the divers countrysides, re-landing on the 29th at Cape Henry and setting up a cross to God, finally sailing on to the island where ill-omened but eternally famous Jamestown was to arise.

❧

It has been only in recent years that proper recognition has been made of that fateful day when these few courageous men *"descried the land of Virginia,"* and *"landed and discovered a little way. . . . "* Then was our nation founded. It is fitting that the commemoration of it has taken the nature of a pilgrimage each April into the sand dunes at the foot of Old Cape Henry Light, where the landing was probably made. And it is as fitting that in 1931 the President of our nation should have attended not as President but as only one of the thousands of humble pilgrims gathered together to give thanks to God.

It has been still more recently that any effort has been made to preserve as a monument this wild and beautiful and hallowed region. But thoughtful men have lately begun efforts in this direction and it may not now be long until it will have been made into a state park passing down through the generations its memories and unchanged majesty.

I tried to love your mountains . . . .

        *   *   *

But I could ever smell the tang
Of great waves breaking, breaking . . . .
And in my ears I ever heard
The sand-dunes calling me.
—John Richard Moreland.

A T dawn, noon or night there is magic in the dunes with the tide licking to their feet up the glistening beach. They are not mere tumbled piles of sand, here bare except for the deep cut carving of the wind, here tangled with sassafrass and jasmine, here crested with plumes of bending grass silhouetted against the sky. They are a presence, a personality on whose countenance is graven deep the lines of ceaseless struggle with wind and sea.

Gulls wheel over the dunes. A sea hawk drifts high and black against the sun. The changing glory of sunset and soft gold of night gleam on the wet sand. Spume, froth from the torn surf, swept in on the forefront of each wave, is tossed by the wind in ghostly grey shadows across the beach. Far away a ship drops below the horizon. In search of food, a family of sandpipers flit in and out of the edge of the water.

Like the tinkling surface notes of a song these things fill the eyes, but ever underneath throbs a giant undertone drowning heart and will in the deep, thrilling melody of dune and sea. . . . And once this siren song has entered your heart, you will never again be free. Neither years nor distance will lessen its hold. Often far away in the worries of little things, that are so big today but so small in the years, like a cool hand a memory of the dune-fringed sea will well up in your mind . . . and bitterness will be swept away as the salt wind murmurs again to the stars, *"What are such little frets to the waves and the dunes . . . to the sea and its changeless tides . . . ?"*

. . . . *little hills*
Of wrinkled sand, where purple shadow-birds
Are poised for flight. The bruised myrtle spills
Its fragrance precious as remembered words
Of other Junes. . . . .

There is no wind, but heady as old wine
This beauty is, that glitters strangely white
Along the sand.

—June Night, John Richard Moreland

YOU MAY NOT LOVE THE DUNES

You may not love the dunes: your eyes may see
Only a waste of sand and oaten grass.
Scorched by the sun, and torn by winds that pass
From dawn to dawn. The ache—the misery
Of blasted trees, the drought and loneliness
You may not love—or humble solitudes,
Shadow and sun and all their changing moods,
Or tiger-winds so wild and pitiless.

But O I love the dunes, I know their ways
Through dark and dazzling hours from June to June;—
The first green flush of April, and the days
Of white December, summer's tortured noon
Scarred with bleached bones . . . Now I am old,
These yellow hills are dear as coined gold.

—John Richard Moreland.

The wind is harrowing the dunes tonight,
It mocks the sea and hisses at the moon,
Bends slender trees, and like a lyric sprite
Plays on the broken reeds a plaintive tune,
And twirls the sand in spirals thin and white . . .
         —Wind on the Dunes, John Richard Moreland.

THERE is no more remarkable thing in all this remarkable region than the Moving Dunes of Cape Henry. Behind the low, thickly grown dunes at the edge of the sea is a forest. Beach and dunes have apparently ended. But suddenly you glimpse through an open space, or through the pines, or towering startlingly above them, an upheaved desert. The sand has not been content to stay by the sea. It has forced its way inshore—and ever aided by the wind marches on year after year.

These high, mysterious dunes can easily be reached from Old Cape Henry Light. After the climb up them, there comes an impression of being no longer near the ocean but in a desert far from shore. The surface is a sea of waves rippled up by the wind. Small knolls are carved into grotesque shapes. Slender swords of grass have somehow found root, and here and there a huckleberry or sassafras bush. Around the tufts of grass finely drawn circles lead to the belief that some geometrically minded phantom has been wandering afoot with a fairy compass—until you discover your error in watching the swordlike blades bent low, and swaying, in the wind.

Standing in this desert, you might laugh if someone should tell you there is a forest beneath, that this tightly graven surface stretches over the tops of thousands of grey, dead trees which once lifted high above the land about. But you will cease to laugh, and will believe, and will mock no more when you top the last high dune and look down over the end of the world. . . .

"One Seeing is worth a hundred Tellings."
—Chinese Proverb.

THE edge of the world! It might better be said the dividing line between Life and the obliterating blankness of Eternity. From the high level of the rolling sands, a steep slope abruptly descends into forest and swamp. It is amazing, impressive, almost unbelievable. Indeed, it may seem almost a mirage until you sit on the rounded edge of the dune and stare for awhile and seek the truth. When you do, there will creep over you the knowledge that this is real; and you will feel Silence, the Silence of great, powerful forces battling too grimly for outcry.

Down in the forest a frog croaks, or a whipoorwill cries his mournful plaint, or a twig crackles. But Silence still presses overwhelmingly into your brain, overpowering it, slowly shrinking you into your tiny role in eternity.

Suddenly a soft swish drifts up from the slope. Startled, you look. It is a tiny landslide slowly widening like molten metal overflowing its crucible. There is a dull hiss as it sifts into the dark marsh-water. The movement dies away. Silence reigns again. . . . And you have witnessed the sands at work. It is this slow, infrequent motion, starting from no apparent impulse—unless it be a fragment of that great forgotten one that in forgotten years first set the dunes on their way—, which fills the swamp at the bottom, crushes the bushes, chokes life from the trees, at last covers them above the highest twig as irresistibly the dunes move on.

Yet as you look out on dead tree tops protruding from the steep slope, on the matted bulwark of live ones at the bottom, on vegetation clinging here and there on the incline, you are still unconvinced and you think, "This is the end. Such a barrier will stop the dunes. I am among the last to see this remarkable thing. Soon grass and shrubs will conquer the sand and the moving wall will be still."

But the dunes heed not. They do not even trouble to scorn. Under them are trees as vital, as thick, as tall. They have heard such little murmurings before through the long years, and know the worth of them in the bounds of Time and unchanging purpose. Today, little rills of sand will slip down; tomorrow, others. When he who thinks the end has come returns another year, he looks in vain for his dead tree tops. They are there, but buried; and the grey, leafless ones he sees now are those that were his living bulwark when last he was here.

Like Time . . . like Life . . . the Dunes move on.

A picture is a poem without words.

—Horace.

THE DESERT back of the moving dunes is a wild and lonely and beautiful wilderness, much of which is low and marshy. Here is Spanish moss filling the air with phantom fingers. Here are long creepers weaving a mesh through the thick-growing trees. Here is black swamp-water never moving except in the silent ripples that flow in widening, dying circles from where a berry or twig has fallen—or in the slow ebb and rise of the seasons. And in winter even these are stilled by the white, cold hand of ice.

At other places, though the forest is as thick, it rises from dry ground. It, too, would be almost impassable were it not for the many miles of trails which you can follow for a day or for week on week exploring as some ancestor may have explored 300 years ago, finding the same primitive wilderness, hearing the same bird and animal cries.

Again, there is the loveliness of trees growing on sand dunes that perhaps marched here over another forest centuries in the past. Most of the tangled lesser vegetation has been choked out. The trees are wide apart and well spaced. It is almost as if man had planted them to give him room to loll and roam as he might will through the long broken avenues of rolling whiteness.

But the perfection of beauty is when by trail or untracked way through the forest you suddenly break clear to blue, sparkling water beneath a dune far inland. The picture shown here is of White Hill. . . . It is only one of many mounds of sand on White Hill Lake or Broad Bay where far from the sea and far from the world you can sit watching shadow and sun on slopes as white as drifted snow, listening to the whisper of little waves brushing to and fro across the rim of a tiny beach.

I will arise and go now, and go to Innisfree,
  *   *   *
And I shall have some peace there, for peace comes dropping
    slow,
Dropping from the veils of morning to where the cricket
    sings;
There midnight's all a-glimmer, and noon a purple glow,

And evening full of the linnet's wings.

I will arise and go now, for always night and day
I hear lake water lapping with low sound by the shore;
While I stand on the roadway, or on the pavement gray,
  I hear it in the deep heart's core.

—The Lake Isle of Innisfree, Yeats.

BOTH in history and the odd ways of Nature the region back of Cape Henry is so unique and outstanding that it would make a park without parallel in the country. There is enchantment in every step of it, in the sea and endless dunes, in the advancing sand and desert, in wilderness and swamp. But, excepting the sea, of all its attractions none can surpass that of its inland waters.

These almost change the Cape into an island. From the deep cleft of Lynnhaven Inlet, Long Creek—the magic stream on the facing page—cuts a narrow, winding course to Broad Bay. It, in turn, runs into Linkhorn Bay which is never very far from the coast and at Crystal Lake and Little Neck Creek approaches so near that hardly more than a quarter of a mile of sand turns back the beating waves of the Atlantic.

The delight of these waters is in visiting them, seeing them, not in hearing of them. But it is interesting here to give space to their possibilities as set forth by Herbert Evison, Executive Secretary of the National Council of State Parks, in his report on the Cape Henry park proposal:

"I feel quite free to say in respect to this that it would meet the most exacting standards established by any state, in every respect—as to extent, scenic quality and suitability for those purposes for which parks are established—recreation in its broadest sense, and education.

"No feature of the area is of greater interest both as to general attractiveness and as to possibilities of useful development than the water area behind the "desert" . . .

"Seen from the air, the bays, extending a considerable distance southward to a point only a few hundred yards from the ocean beach, reveal their development possibilities almost instantly. Here, given a cleared and reasonably direct channel, is such an anchorage as yachtsmen might dream about, sheltered, extensive, offering ready access not only to the proposed park area but also to the resorts of Virginia Beach; an opportunity for canoeing and . . . motorboating."

*"What shall we do but climb the world to peep
beyond the wall!"*

So we come back to the sea again.

Beginning with Old Cape Henry Light this part of the book has tried to tell a little of the cape shore and hinterland which fall within the bounds of the suggested State Park. Although there is witchery in these pictures and a hundred others for which there was no space here, and in Moreland's poems, these are after all but the shadow of the real. Whatever magic their beauty may have for you, it too is but the shadow of the overwhelming spell this great duneland will fasten upon your heart once you have wandered into it.

Yet the sea will always call you back again. After dark, mirrored waters; after tangled, shadowy forest; after gloomy swamp and the soft swish of sand ever trickling down on its steady march inland—after day on day of returning to the enchantment of this hinterland, you will mount once more in slow, sliding steps the mysterious, creeping slope of the Moving Dunes to come face to face with blue water. Once more you will feel the tang of salt winds blowing. Once more you will know that whatever else there may be here it is the sea whose presence, hanging over sand and forest and lake, has charged this capeland with something of its own eternal, restless questing after the mysterious . . . the far . . . the unknown and unachieved.

And just a stone's throw further on
One came upon the sea.
—Newry, John Richard Moreland.

WIND AND SEA

The wind is a teasing hunger,
   The sea is a quenchless thirst,
And I am a moon-marked dreamer
   By wind and wave accursed;—

With never a place to linger,
   Or hide from the seeking sea,
But the curve of a thin, blue finger
   Continually beckons me.

With never a hill or hollow
   To harbor me safe and sure,
But the wind, hound-like, will follow
   And sniff at my bolted door.

Or set the casement shaking
   Till quiet or rest is vain,
Till the sound of water . . . breaking . . .
   Makes me its slave again.

—*John Richard Moreland.*

. . . . *the sea*
* * *
Where the ships of youth are running
 Close-hauled on the edge of the wind
With all adventure before them
 And only the old behind.
—Humbert Wolfe.

WHATEVER the magic of the shore and far-off ports, he who loves the sea returns to it and voyages out again on its trackless ways. To him it is not a broad highway leading him to the sands or harbors of other coasts, but the road of his life. The cities and allurements of land, even the content of a house and the nearness of those he loves as he comes home from the sea, are only ports of call, only places to linger awhile as with dreamy eyes he watches his ship tugging restlessly at its cable with each flow of the outbound tide. The time always comes when he can watch no longer. However dear to him, he must slip the moorings that bind his bursting heart and sail again to "the wind's ways and the gull's ways" . . . "and the ways that cannot be told."

"The sea's the sailor's home, and it's there he'll be found on the ultimate day," said Trader Horn as he remembered his rivers of Africa like green snakes with bellies of silver winding down to the sea. And there is a lonely, wistful, beautiful chorus that may sometimes be heard echoing in the dusk from the golden blurs of windows fringing a bay where ships lie waiting for the ebbing of the tide at dawn:

"Old sailors nev-er die . . . nev-er die . . . nev-er die . . .
Old sailors nev-er die . . .
They just sail . . . away."

The harbor-bay was clear as glass,
So smoothly was it strewn!
And on the bay the moonlight lay
And the shadow of the moon.
And the bay was white with silent light
                    *   *   *

                            —The Ancient Mariner.

"I LOVE ALL THINGS THAT CLUSTER AROUND THE SEA"

I love all things that cluster around the sea,
Sand-dunes wave washed, and wild, glad wings that beat
Against the wind, the flash of children's feet,
Rude, huddled huts, driftwood, grass blowing free,
Seines in the sun and spars of hickory,
Great ships slow moving, and boats small and neat,
Old mossy wrecks that once were trim and fleet
Half hidden by a pine or bayberry tree.

But when the tired feet have homeward gone,
And from the huts blue smoke curls toward the sky,
And yellow lights gleam on the waters gray,
There comes a peace as soothing as the dawn
As silently the little boats go by
And drop their anchors in the quiet bay.

—*John Richard Moreland.*

. · . . days run
As fast away as does the sun.
—Robert Herrick.

ND - #0126 - 020323 - C0 - 229/152/4 - PB - 9780259506416 - Gloss Lamination